SCOTT

Signs
of a Great Résumé

How to Write a Résumé that Speaks for Itself

Illustrations by Kenny Durkin.
Author photo courtesy of C. Stephenson Photography.

For more information, news about upcoming events and
other !@#$% publications, visit:

www.ScottVedder.com
ISBN: 1475291841
ISBN-13: 9781475291841

Signs of Great Gratitude

Thank you to the family, friends, colleagues and leaders who have been my mentors, my teachers and my motivation along this journey. I'm forever grateful for your love and support. And certainly, thank you to the well-meaning job seekers whose amusing résumé antics were my inspiration.

To my mother, Cathy Vedder, whose classic line *"So you're gonna go in there..."* helped me learn early in life that great preparation for a job search is critical. She's done far more for me than I could ever write about in just a few lines.

To my father, Warren Vedder, whose tireless dedication to his family meant many long work days for him so that we could enjoy the quality of life he felt we deserved. His line:*"You think you know but you don't know,"* taught me to always keep learning and to question convention.

To my brother, Jay Vedder, who followed his heart to pursue a career that he loved. The compassion, dedication, humor and intellect he uses on the job have also made him my best friend. *"We're your friends 'till the bitter end..."* He makes me laugh like no one else and has quite a knack for proofreading.

To my partner, Antonio Tapia, Esq., whose eye for innovation, entrepreneurial success and spirit to fight for what he wants to achieve have inspired me to keep growing and to push myself to new heights. (He's also one hell of an editor!) *"May I encourage you...?"* Yes Tony... you may.

Table of Contents

1

PUT ON A HAPPY PREFACE

Hi! Thanks for reading! You're already one step closer to finding a great new job. This book is the culmination of experience I gained at my job as a recruiter at a Fortune 100 company. There I interviewed people just like you. Well, maybe not **exactly** like you, but each with a similar goal in mind: to get a great new job.

My goal in writing this book is not only to prepare you for your job quest but also I hope to inform you, produce great results and even make you smile along the way. In fact, those were my goals in every interview I conducted.

In interviews I like to make people laugh. I make people laugh because let's face it, interviews are uncomfortable. I try to break down the barrier between me, the intimidating interviewer behind the big desk, and someone like you, the applicant. I also make people laugh so I can do a tooth check – good dental hygiene is a must! Just kidding… but seriously, I want my applicants to be comfortable so they can be themselves in the interview.

I also want you to be comfortable so that **you** can be yourself on your résumé. I'm going to give you tools that will enable you to showcase why **YOU** are the best applicant for the job. To many, writing a résumé is boring and tedious. Hopefully I'll make it as fun as possible. And to show you that I'm serious about having fun with résumés, let me start by sharing my favorite joke:

(I'm actually laughing while typing this.)

Two résumés are sitting in a stack of papers.
One of them says, "Holy cow, it's crowded in here!"
The other one says, "Holy cow, a talking résumé!"

I bet you <u>can't</u> <u>wait</u> to get started doing this résumé business with a fun guy like me! We're on our way to finding you a rewarding, financially beneficial new job and hopefully you're already laughing.

So enough about me – let's talk about you. I'll bet you're somebody who wants a new job, a better job, more money or just a new opportunity. Join the club! I'll bet you also want flexible hours, great benefits, free travel and a company car too. Great! You've already taken the first step towards those goals… ambition! You have high hopes, great goals and the drive to begin your journey.

Now how exactly do you get there?

Well before you get the travel perks and the company car, you're going to have to **earn** an interview by submitting a great résumé. For many people, the idea of summarizing their entire career on one sheet of paper is very intimidating.

Have no fear! In this book, you've got all of the tools you need to craft an effective résumé that speaks for itself. Many of the other résumé books already out there are *hundreds* of pages long. They are filled with useless examples of what hypothetical résumés *might* look like. "Jane Doe wants to be a Sales Manager." "John Doe wants to be an astronaut." How does all of that help you? – It probably doesn't.

There are even services that charge hundreds of dollars to write résumés. If you had that kind of money lying around, you probably wouldn't have picked up a book about résumés. If I had that kind of money lying around, I probably wouldn't have written one!

If you went for one of those résumé books, I'll bet you were confused by whether to use a functional résumé, a blended résumé, a chronological résumé or maybe none at all. What I'm going to do is to simplify things for you with what I call the Signs of a Great Résumé.

While **!**, @, **#**, **$**, and **%** might look like a substitute for curse words in a comic strip, you'll soon learn how they're actually the simplest way to make your résumé shine. I've taken some of the best tools of the trade and my real life experience gained through conducting over 5,000 interviews and presented them here for you.

Before we start, you'll have to learn what a résumé really is. Your résumé is your personal professional advertisement. You're trying to get a prospective employer to buy a great product and that great product is your experience! You've made the investment, (or at least have started looking at this book inside the bookstore - you thief) so let's get started!

2

SIGN LANGUAGE

So why exactly do I call this book Signs of a Great Résumé? You'll notice that I use the signs !, @, #, $ and % throughout the book. Right now they may look like a substitute for curse words in a comic strip and I admit that writing a résumé could certainly drive some people to curse. But by the end of this book these signs are going to be your friends. So let's get familiar with them.

Each sign represents an important part of a successful résumé and each has its own job to do. They'll be easier to understand by the end of this book but if you ever forget, remembering them is as simple as looking at the keys of the first five numbers on your keyboard. I'll bet you just looked at your keyboard, didn't you?… see what I mean? The 1 has an !, the 2 has an @, the 3 has a # and so on. So when it comes to writing a résumé, what do they mean? Let's have a look…

From now on, almost every single word that you write into your résumé should relate to one of these signs. If you're not using these signs, you're not being specific enough. If you're not being specific, why should an employer hire **you** specifically? Use these signs often. They'll help your résumé speak for itself in front of a potential employer and will make you stand out from the rest of the applicants.

!

The first sign is an exclamation point. An exclamation point really isn't much of a point at all – it's more like a baseball bat.

Do you see it? It's actually *shaped* like a baseball bat! And when it comes to knocking a résumé out of the park, it's your key to a home run. (Pun intended.) ! represents any part of your experience that was amazing!, totally unique! or one of a kind! Look for **!** achievements throughout your experience and keep them handy for when it's their turn at bat.

In the Self-Interview chapter, we'll talk more about the specific ! achievements you'll want to look out for. Here's a few questions to get you thinking:

What did you do to WOW! people?
What did you do the BEST! compared to others?
What did your boss say was GREAT! about your work?

And finally, don't ever ***actually*** write ! at the end of a sentence. You want to convey the quality of the work you did, without sounding like you're yelling the words on your résumé!!! (See what I mean?)

@

The next sign is an @. You probably recognize this sign from your email address. It's actually an abbreviation for the word "at." C'mon… You've got to hand it to whoever came up with a symbol that is meant to eliminate the need to write a TWO LETTER word!

On your résumé you'll use the meaning behind the sign, but not the actual symbol, to define points in your career when you took certain steps and also for places, dates and things. For example:

@ which school did you get your education?
@ which company did you work?
@ what phone number can you be reached?
@ what mailing address can you be contacted?
@ what dot-com can you be emailed?
(Yes, of course you can use the symbol for your email address.)

Start thinking about some of these questions now. We'll come back to this sign in the Self-Interview chapter.

#

You might not know that the clever little number sign is so special that it even inspired its own game: tic-tac-toe. It's true… ok, maybe not. You're probably thinking "Didn't we just cover phone numbers and addresses with the @ sign?" You're right. But in this book and on your résumé, the # sign represents numbers that quantify and prove your past successes.

Think about these questions:

With what # of customers did you interact?
What # of people did you work with or supervise?
For what # of tasks were you responsible?
What # of sales did you generate?
What # of hours did you volunteer?

This might make it easy to remember; the # sign is also known as the "pound" sign. So think about it this way, the numbers we're talking about with the # sign help give weight to your achievements.

$

All businesses are interested in money. From hedge funds to non-profits, everyone wants more of it. There's an old saying: "Money talks and…" well, you know how it ends. Let money do the talking for you on your résumé. Show your prospective employer the money! Consider these questions:

How much $ did you make for your company?
How much $ did your sales generate?
How much $ did your idea save?
What $ value was the grant you were awarded?
What was the $ value of your contributions?
(Not your salary, which NEVER goes on a traditional résumé.)

%

Have you noticed that the percent sign kinda looks like the number 100? It's how a 100 might appear after a few too many times on a wild carnival ride. Maybe it's doing yoga? Well either way, the % sign really is no mystery; it means percent.

Percentages are great to use on your résumé because they're easy to understand. They're a simple way to show change, performance and other factors that make your work stand out. It's one thing to say you sold 200 donkeys, but it sounds much better to say that you sold 300% *more* donkeys than last year. By using a %, you've shown that you can really work your ass off. (Sorry, couldn't resist the pun.)

Think about these questions:

By what % did your personal performance improve?
What % increase in results did you generate?
What % of the unnecessary work did you eliminate?
What % of the total revenues did you bring in?
What % of your clients came back year after year?

! @ # $ %

So now you're a little more fluent in "sign" language. Using the signs you learned about in this chapter you'll be able to draft a résumé that speaks for itself. Later on, we're going to revisit each one of these signs in the Self-Interview chapter. But in the meantime keep thinking about them as you move through the book. Let's get to work!

3

A RÉSUMÉ IS NOT A JOB DESCRIPTION (AND OTHER COMMON MISTAKES)

Thomas Edison once said, "Genius is one percent inspiration and ninety nine percent perspiration." Actually, he probably said it more than once – but I digress. Even though many candidates sweat bullets before an interview, that's not the perspiration that Edison was talking about. Of course what he meant was hard work. In my case, the ninety nine percent perspiration comes from the hard work I put into conducting over 5,000 interviews over the years; some of them were great and some of them were not so great. These interviews led to my one percent inspiration for this book. I wanted to write a book to help people overcome common mistakes in résumé writing and give them the tools to make a résumé that speaks for itself. No sweat.

Let's talk about some of these common mistakes now. The number one mistake I see in my experience are résumés that read like a job description. What I mean is that lots of people tend to simply list the basic functions and responsibilities of their previous positions, but they never tell the recruiter how they performed, what they accomplished and what made their experience better than everyone else. Take a look below for examples of how the Signs of a Great Résumé helped this teacher write a résumé that went straight to the head of the class.

Before using Signs of a Great Résumé	After using Signs of a Great Résumé
Taught English classes.	Taught four unique courses at Memorial Middle School including advanced English, Literature and Composition with classes up to 24 students.
Graded papers and tracked grades.	Reviewed over 200 assignments each week. Designed a grade tracking system that increased input efficiency by 50%.
Prepared students for next grade.	Successfully prepared students to enter high school with a pass rate of 98%, an increase of 2% over the previous year. This reduced remedial summer school costs by nearly $8,000.

The examples in the left column just list the job description of a teacher. How boring. The examples in the right column use the Signs of a Great Résumé. They provide much more detail about the candidate, showcase improvements in the classroom and highlight key skills that make the résumé speak for itself. They list ! accomplishments like designing a new tracking system and increasing graduation rates. They show @ what school the teacher worked. They include #s of students, papers and classes. They highlight $ saved. They also describe some facts in % making them easy to understand.

You see, using the Signs of a Great Résumé makes all the difference. Again, I can't stress enough:

A RÉSUMÉ IS <u>NOT</u> A JOB DESCRIPTION

Here's another real world example. Let's say I'm a recruiter for a fast-food company and I'm looking to promote a front-line employee to a management role. Each interested candidate submits a résumé. Now it's highly likely that each of them would have similar training and experience that qualified them for the promotion. Because they're coming from a similar background, training and skill set, it's almost certain that I'm going to see the exact same information from résumé to résumé. This is particularly true if they're not using the Signs of a Great Résumé and *always* true if résumés are written like job descriptions. Here are some examples. You'll easily see how all of them look alike.

BAD EXAMPLES:

Employee #1:
• Worked as a cashier, cook and drive through attendant.
• Counted change and processed credit cards

- Learned the computer system for the cash register and trained new employees to use it.

Employee #2:
- Performed positions throughout the restaurant including cashier, grill cook and car-side service.
- Handled cash and credit cards for many customers each day.
- Trainer for new associates, demonstrating the various functions of the computer system.

So which employee should get the promotion? Who knows!?! Although each résumé is unique to the individual, they're both almost exactly the same. Each reads very much like a job description for the front line position. Presenting information this way on your résumé makes it very difficult for your résumé to stand out to a recruiter.

Put yourself in a recruiter's shoes. Imagine for a moment that you were going through hundreds of résumés. You don't know anything else about the candidates and you've never even met them. It would be nearly impossible for you to identify the best candidate if all they offered was a job description on their résumé. Remember, it's the employer's responsibility to give a job description in the job posting. It's the applicant's job to respond by showing how their experience is unique and how they are qualified to fulfill the requirements of the posting. Use the Signs of a Great Résumé and you'll give your recruiter a résumé that speaks for itself.

So one last time, I'll say:

A RÉSUMÉ IS <u>NOT</u> A JOB DESCRIPTION!

Here's another way to look at it. A résumé is an advertisement for a great product: YOU. Think about this. If a hotel runs an ad on television, the ad wouldn't simply tell you you'll have to check in and check out, you have to pay each night and someone will clean your room daily. Everyone should already know these basic elements about what it's like to stay in a hotel. That ad probably wouldn't make you real excited to choose that hotel.

Imagine instead if the hotel ad used the Signs of a Great Résumé. It would talk about a ! cutting edge renovation it just underwent, @ what distance it's located from great local attractions, the # of restaurants it has, the $ room rate discounts available and perhaps the % of satisfied customers that gave it a great review. Look what a difference the Signs of a Great Résumé make! What kind of an "advertisement" are you presenting for your experience and skills?

Here's how you know if your résumé is a great advertisement for you. Take your résumé and cover your name at the top. Without your name, could your résumé belong to someone else? Would most people who held your previous job write what you wrote? If the answers to these questions are yes, then you need to add more specifics that set you apart from the competition.

Got it? Good. Moving on…

———

Here's a few more common mistakes that I've seen on résumés and job applications over the years.

Edit Before You Print —

I've seen countless résumés with white-out, cross-outs, pencil marks and all the other sorts of bad corrections one can imagine. Once when an applicant handed me a résumé covered in scratch outs and corrections, I asked why he made so many changes.

"I just wanted to make sure you had the right information," said the applicant.

"Then why didn't you type it that way in the first place?" I thought to myself. – Be sure your résumé is presentation quality and not a draft or a work in progress. If your résumé isn't ready for an interview, your recruiter might question if you're ready the job.

No Photos Please —

Not long ago a man brought in a mimeographed résumé. Not photo-copied or scanned, but actually done on a mimeograph machine, which he presumably found in a museum somewhere. This mimeographed document also had a grainy picture of himself pasted (in the glued sense of the word "pasted") at the top of the page. Recruiters some-times feel that photos are an applicant's way of indicating race, gender, beauty, fashion sense and other types of char-acteristics that have nothing to do with a person's ability to perform a job. – Leave the pictures to your photo album and the mimeographs to history.

Scrap the Scrapbooking Paper –

Several times I've seen purple paper with purple font. It's lovely to look at but belongs in a scrapbook, and not in a job application. It's nearly impossible to read and definitely difficult to scan or copy. If a recruiter tries to copy or scan your colorful résumé, lots of the information you worked hard to write will be lost into a blurry, black blot. The only place that résumé will be sent is into the recycle bin. I'm sure that like me, most recruiters **hate** "cutesy" paper tricks. Your qualifications should be special, not the hoity-toity paper you use. – A thicker stock of paper is fine and won't wrinkle, but all other paper tricks should be saved for your origami class.

Waste of Space –

A lovely lady gave me a résumé that was divided into two columns up and down the page, sort of like a newspaper. The left-hand column which took up 2/3 of the page was completely blank, except for the word "RÉSUMÉ." (By the way, the word résumé should never *actually* appear on your résumé.) The right 1/3 of the page had a 30 year career cramped into it in really small font. This was not very helpful in terms of my eyesight or in terms of my decision to hire her. What a waste of space. – Columns should be left to the ancient Romans. Exercise good space planning and be mindful of your font size.

Sometimes Less is More –

A college graduate had been working for about ten years and his résumé was **thirteen** pages long! That's more than one page per year! With all that paper inside, his file was so heavy I could barely carry it back to my desk, nonetheless actually read all of that information before his interview. If your résumé reads more like a book than this book does, you probably need to do some editing. Later on, we'll talk about what kinds of information can be left off your résumé.

Lock Down! –

An applicant listed periods of unemployment on his job application as "Prison." Sadly, this was listed multiple times! There's a time and place to talk about criminal backgrounds; your résumé is not that place. – Keep evidence of your time in the lock up locked down and off of your résumé. Understand local laws regarding what you must disclose about your criminal history. For now, don't list anything on your résumé that doesn't help you to get hired.

Barking Up the Wrong Tree –

One cheerful applicant wrote the types of dogs she owned and their names. Even if your pet's name is "Hire Me," I would leave it off.

Keep it Clean –

Your résumé is no place for sexual innuendo or jokes. I've seen email addresses galore that looked more like they belonged on a dating website than on a résumé. The most egregious I've seen was a young man with an email address that included a pretty blatant sexual reference. As you can imagine, this otherwise qualified candidate was not hired. This represented a lack of judgment that made me doubt his ability to interface appropriately with customers and employees. Make sure your email address and anything else that you include on your résumé is professional and appropriate. Keep it classy.

All in the Family –

While it's likely that you're very proud of your family, writing about them is not appropriate on a résumé. An applicant wrote the names, ages and social security numbers of all his children on his résumé. He had three, by the way, and several "wonderful" grand children. I'm not sure why on earth he thought an employer would need this. In fact, many recruiters might frown upon this as an attempt to leverage family connections in order to get a job. Neither your social security number nor anyone else's should ever appear on a traditional résumé. If you want to showcase your family, join the PTA.

"T.M.I." –

Sometimes too much information is just no good; certain jobs you've held might be best left off of a résumé. I once interviewed a young woman who said she held several "entertainment" jobs. On her résumé she listed her job title as "stripper." Under this title, she listed her responsibilities as "Keeping gentlemen company." Needless to say, she was not applying for that kind of role so it really stood out for all the wrong reasons. You're not required to list every single job you ever held on a résumé. Even though this example seems a little extreme, this advice goes for everyone. Only list jobs that have prepared you for or relate directly to the role for which you're currently applying. If you list too many unrelated jobs, you may seem to lack focus in your career, that you switch jobs too often or that you might be apt to leave a job quickly. You want to paint a cohesive picture of someone on a clear path to success in the role for which you're applying. Strip your experience down to the bare essentials.

"Pubic" Enemy Number One –

This one's my personal favorite and actually came to my mother's desk, but it was well worth stealing the story to tell it to you here. My mother was the Executive Secretary at a small-town library. The job posting was for the Library Director. One well-educated gentleman, with a degree in Library Science, proudly stated on his résumé that he had extensive experience dealing with the pubic. Yep, you read that right… the pubic. He went to school specifically to learn how to run a library and since then he claimed he has only dealt with people from the waist down. Remember that spell check doesn't replace common sense and some-times gives a false sense of security. Proofread, proofread, proofread!

As you can see, you're not the only one out there who needs a little help writing a résumé. Take the time to scan your résumé for these common mistakes. Although these errors can make a recruiter's life more entertaining, they over-shadow the qualifications of an otherwise perfect candi-date. Because they're so easy to catch and correct, there's no excuse for having them on your résumé from now on.

4

SPEED DATING

You never get a second chance to make a first impression. In that way, reviewing résumés is kind of like speed dating. Your résumé will probably be reviewed for somewhere between seven and thirty seconds before a recruiter makes the decision to give you a closer look or move along. He's kind of like an eligible bachelor looking for his perfect match. Those few precious moments can make or break *your* career.

Finding the perfect match for a job opening is a bit like sorting through potential mates at a singles bar. Everyone's looking for "Mr. or Ms. Right." You only have a limited amount of time to catch a recruiter's eye. To do this, your résumé needs to speak to the recruiter using concise and simple phrasing. On a résumé you need to state the most important facts before you lose the recruiter's attention. If you think of it like speed dating, you've got lots of folks to look at, but no time to hear their life story. You want to be the one who gets a call the next day, so keep it short and sweet.

Here's a quick exercise to demonstrate my point. Take a look at the following paragraph for seven seconds… ok, make it ten, and see what you can remember. GO!

I have been working in several different fields including some types of agricultural and biotechnical design. I bred dogs, cats, hamsters, gerbils, hermit crabs, gold fish, elephants, and guinea pigs. My next company manufactured artificial apples, made primarily of velvet, generally of the Granny Smith variety. I also started a new way of making the apples using exclusively organic compounds upon which to adhere the velvet, a first in the industry.

How much of that did you remember? If you read it for only ten seconds, probably not a whole lot. Now read this information:

ELEPHANT BREEDER

• Experience breeding 12 species of domestic and exotic animals including African elephants.

VELVET APPLE MAKER

• Manufactured velvet Granny Smith apples. Created the world's first organic velvet apples.

In the second version, you could read both statements within ten seconds. And you likely gained a lot more information about this theoretical person's odd experience because they gave a great first impression with a quick snapshot of their experience. You didn't have to read a whole paragraph to figure out what they did. The second example employs the use of some of the Signs of a Great Résumé.

You likely don't know much about making Velvet Apples. Did the first example help you understand that experience? If you were a recruiter, that paragraph probably wouldn't have caught your eye. Rather than read something about potentially unrelated experience, a recruiter would rather move on to the next résumé.

This highlights how using direct and simple phrasing can make your life and your recruiter's life a lot easier. You'll write less and they'll learn more. It'll be love at first sight.

SIGN TIME

! – Your résumé should contain anything that might make the recruiter say "Wow!" You should not **actually** use the exclamation point as punctuation in your résumé. It can help to emphasize a point, but if you put it at the end of a sentence, it sometimes feels like you're yelling at someone. RIGHT?!?!

5

SET UP FOR SUCCESS

Now we're ready to get started writing the first draft of your résumé. By that I mean a good old fashioned paper résumé to bring with you to interviews. Even though it's likely you're also going to need a résumé in electronic format (i.e. a web-based job posting, an online application, etc.), it is always best to draft your résumé in a printable format first. Doing this will help you use the Signs of a Great Résumé to describe your most valuable experience in one concise document. Once you have a paper résumé it's easy to adapt it into an electronic format later-on as needed. Besides, it's always important to show up with a paper résumé in a face-to-face interview… but we'll have to cover interviews in another book. (Hint, hint.) So let's get your printable résumé set up for success.

Imagine that every square inch of your paper résumé is like valuable beachfront real estate. You don't want to waste any space. If there's something unnecessary on your "real estate," then evict it off the page. Here's a few tips that will start you on your way:

• **Blank Page:** Don't use any fancy formats or pre-made templates for your résumé. Start with a blank page. A blank page may seem intimidating, but after reading this book, you'll have the tools you need to successfully bring that blank page to life with ease. Do not draw lines, use text boxes or insert pictures onto the page.

• **Font:** Using a simple, classic font like Times New Roman or Arial is really the way to go. Use the same font everywhere on your résumé. Simple fonts are easy on the eyes and take up less space than others. Typically 12-point Times or 10-point Arial is easy for most people to read when printed. If you go any smaller you're probably cramming too much unnecessary information into your résumé and you may be causing the recruiter to feel old if they need their reading glasses to see what you've written.

Avoid italics. Italicizing makes your font smaller and harder to read. (Yeah. I know. You've seen me using italics throughout this book. But this is a *book*, not a *résumé*.)

• **Margins:** Keep your margins between .5 and 1 inch for the top, bottom, left, and right. That should give you some valuable extra space, but will still be within the print margins of most printers. Double-check that it prints correctly of course and adjust the margins as needed.

- **Creative Space:** Notice that earlier I said 10 or 12 point font were the easiest text sizes to read. That's true. However, I never said your blank lines had to be that big. Highlight any blank lines on your résumé and lower the font size to gain some extra space. You'll see the height of the blank lines change as you adjust the font size. In a pinch I've gone as low as 3 point but most blank lines look fine when set to 8 point font. Do this a few times and you'll get to add a few extra lines of content onto the page. It buys you additional real estate without cramping your style.

You can also save a lot of room by putting only one space after each period. Additionally try moving around your bullets and line returns on a page. These nifty little tricks will save you even more space.

SIGN TIME

! – Your experience and qualifications should make your recruiter say "Wow**!**" not your paper. Don't use any letterhead, colored, watermarked or grainy paper. Stick with a high quality, plain white paper. A slightly heavier or thicker paper is fine, but leave the papyrus to the ancient Egyptians.

6

WHAT'S IN A NAME?

You would think that putting your name and contact information on a résumé is so basic that anyone can do it. Well anyone **can** do it, but surprisingly, not everyone can do it correctly.

First of all, your name should be bigger than the rest of your font, but not enormous. If I'm using 12 point font for the body of the résumé I generally bump up the name to 16 point, bold it and center it on the page. I commonly use all caps to further differentiate it. Put your address on the next line then add your email address and phone number.

If you have a name that is gender ambiguous, and you'd like to avoid confusion, you may consider utilizing a title such as Mr. Jamie Smith or Ms. Pat Johnson.

Lots of folks like to add letters to the ends of their names. This is typically appropriate for people with professional degrees or licensures such as Ph.D., M.D., R.N., C.P.A. or Esq.

Education and training at all levels are important personal accomplishments; but not all deserve a spot next to your name. For example, if you have an Associate of Arts degree, great. However, it's not typical and doesn't help to put "A.A." after your name. The same goes for courses or certifications that you may have taken and mean something in your field. However these aren't traditionally included when stating your name. These may include LMT for Licensed Massage Therapist, PHR for Professional of Human Resources, EMT for Emergency Medical Technician and many more. Some of those additional letters may cause you to appear that you're trying too hard and will stand out for the wrong reasons.

Similarly, if you have proudly served the country in the military, it's certainly something that can be mentioned in your résumé. However, unless you're applying for another government job, your rank should not appear as part of your name.

Your additional qualifications, training and certifications are all items that can be included elsewhere in your résumé and we'll talk about that later on. For now keep it simple.

First let's look at what not to do. For whatever reason, many people seem to list their names in some variation of the following format:

BAD EXAMPLE:

Your Name, L.M.N.O.Q.   123 Main Street
                                      Any City, ST ZIP
                                      yourname@_.com
                                      555-555-5555

I don't know why some people think that recruiters like to see fancy shaded boxes or pretty lines. In fact, many text boxes and lines do not transfer appropriately to online job posting systems or become illegible when copied or scanned. So you should avoid them altogether. Remember to just start with a blank page and go from there.

GOOD EXAMPLES:

Your Name

123 Main Street, Any City, ST ZIP
yourname@_.com – 555-555-5555

YOUR NAME, M.D.
123 Main Street, Any City, ST ZIP
555-555-5555 - yourname@_.com

These examples showcase your name in a simple, professional manner and put it front and center for the recruiter to remember. The address and information are legible but are not focal points on the page.

SIGN TIME

@ - Make sure that you put an accurate and appropriate email address. I recommend something like:

yourname@whatever_domain_you_choose.com.

If you don't have that as your current email address, simply create a new one. There are many ways to obtain a new email address for free. Use a well-known domain or your own domain if you have your own site that you wouldn't mind a prospective employer visiting. Do not use your current company's email address if you're posting outside of that company. Don't get too fancy or creative with underscores, symbols or numbers either. Just use your first and last name which is always appropriate and keeps it simple.

I advocate that you create a new email address and that you use this email address ONLY for job postings. That way you avoid your recruiter stumbling across your social network site or anything else that your current email is linked to on the internet that you don't want them to see.

7

OBJECTIVE: WRITE A BETTER OBJECTIVE

Lots of folks have an objective written on their résumé that says something like this:

BAD EXAMPLE:

Objective: To find a challenging position with a growing company that will utilize my skills and experience and enable me to grow a successful career while being developed both personally and professionally.

Yawn. A good percentage of the résumés I've seen contain this boring, uninteresting and mundane sentence or some form of it. It surprises me that so many people seem to think this is the best way to open their personal professional advertisement. The above example uses a lot of words to say nothing at all. You should remember from the "Speed Dating" chapter that your résumé may only be reviewed for a few seconds on average. You don't want those precious seconds wasted here.

SIGNS OF A GREAT RÉSUMÉ

Remember the whole point of Signs of a Great Résumé is to make a résumé that speaks for itself. Yours won't if it uses the same bland objective statement that everyone else is using.

If you're applying for a job, your objective is already clear: to get *that* job. On your résumé you should keep your objective that simple. This helps out a potentially busy, overworked or disorganized recruiter who may have several openings for which you could be applying. Listing the specific title of the job helps eliminate the possibility of your résumé ending up in the wrong pile.

Simply state the name of the exact job that you want as your objective. If there's a position number listed on the job posting, you can include that too if you'd like. So the objective that you write on every résumé should look like this:

OBJECTIVE: (Title of the job for which you're applying.)

It's that simple. Again, think about the "Set Up For Success" chapter where we talked about the value of the real estate on your résumé. This little beauty takes up just one line and it helps clearly define for which job you're applying. It also proves that you've customized your résumé for that posting and that you're not just sending out blanket résumés with no direction; which by the way, you should never do.

Here are some examples of effectively written objectives:

OBJECTIVE: Sales Representative - Position #42099

OBJECTIVE: Fifth Grade Elementary School Teacher

36

OBJECTIVE: Assistant Manager of International Sales

OBJECTIVE: Funeral Director

OBJECTIVE: Donut Hole Cutter

OBJECTIVE: Writer of a Phenomenal Résumé Book

…Get the idea?

By now your résumé should look something like this:

Your Name
123 Main Street Any City, ST
yourname@ .com – 555-555-5555

OBJECTIVE:
(Title of the job for which you're applying.)

8

RÉSUMÉS ARE BLIND – THEY HAVE NO I's

Before you write anything else on your résumé, you'll have to learn a bit about the language of résumés. A résumé, unlike most other forms of writing, should be written in fragmented sentences that get to the point immediately. You also should not write a résumé in the first person. That means you'll need to drop the word "I" from most of your sentences and re-write them.

Consider the following statement:

BAD EXAMPLE:

I am a construction manager. I supervise a group of employees who build new homes.

Now think about rephrasing that statement with a fragment that removes the first-person point-of-view. Remember to use the Signs of a Great Résumé.

GOOD EXAMPLE:

Managed construction of new luxury homes.
Led a team of 29 employees.

These examples both essentially say the same thing, but the second is more effective in conveying the experience of the construction manager.

To keep the voice of the résumé consistent throughout, write everything in the past tense. Even if you're writing about your current job, as long as you did something yesterday or earlier, you've done it in the past.

Here's another example:

BAD EXAMPLE:

I answer phones at a call center and sell products to customers. My weekly goal is $10,000. I usually sell about 5% over goal each week.

Now let's rephrase that information and throw in some more facts that include the Signs of a Great Résumé for good measure.

GOOD EXAMPLE:

Responded to over 75 inbound sales calls daily.
Regularly exceeded $10k weekly sales goal by 5% or higher.

You can see how using fragments helps to keep things simple but also conveys more detailed information to the recruiter. We now have a clear picture of how many calls this representative received and how well he or she performed.

9

COMING SOON TO A RÉSUMÉ NEAR YOU

In the "Speed Dating" chapter, we premiered the importance of using clear and concise phrasing. In movie terms, I guess you'd call that chapter the prequel. In this chapter I'm going to teach you to hone those skills while writing a section titled the Summary of Qualifications, the "teaser trailer" for your résumé.

The Summary of Qualifications is like the coming attractions for a movie. Movie studios produce quick, compelling trailers and previews because when you see the highlights of a movie, you want to go see the entire film. The same goes for your résumé. The recruiter is your captive audience that will watch your teaser trailer for about seven to thirty seconds. In that brief time, you want to convince him that your résumé is a blockbuster hit and that **you** are the right star for the role.

Most people's résumés are full of long sentences and paragraphs that leave the reader only to guess where to find the best information. Hidden between lines that read like job descriptions and other generally boring information are the real gems of many applicants' experience.

See how long it takes you to find the most valuable information in the following paragraph. See if you can figure out why someone should hire this person.

BAD EXAMPLE:

Large Department Store Company – Sales Associate
Any City, ST - 1990 to 2007

Worked in a variety of positions for a major national retailer. Sold merchandise in menswear, shoes, luggage, jewelry and household departments. Trained new employees on the computer system and on approved sales techniques. Worked on a commission basis and provided excellent service. Personally designed a sales competition that resulted in a 50% increase in sock sales. Folded shirts and pants from the returns near the dressing room.

If you were a recruiter with hundreds of résumés to read, you probably would have lost interest around the word "jewelry." This paragraph is about as exciting as a silent film documentary. There's no vivid dialogue or explosive pops that make it interesting. It doesn't quickly tell you anything unique about the "star of the show," the applicant. However, there is some great information tucked into the fifth sentence. It took me about 15 seconds of reading to even get to that sentence. I had passed the seven-second threshold long before then. If this was a movie trailer, I'd be at the popcorn stand instead of watching it.

Imagine if instead of that bulky paragraph the beginning of this candidate's résumé, right after his or her objective, contained this much simpler statement:

GOOD EXAMPLE:

Over 15 years of front-line sales experience at a national retailer. Implemented sales program which increased revenues by 50%.

Doesn't that catch your attention? Doesn't it make you want to know more about this person? Won't you buy a ticket to that movie? Here's another example.

BAD EXAMPLE:

Deb's Debits Accounting Firm – Junior Accountant
Big City, ST – Jan. 2006 to Mar. 2012

Performed various accounting functions at this large firm in a major city. Managed day-to-day transactions and operational details of two dozen accounts with a total value of over $200k. Completed many special projects including working with an outside company on an overhaul of the client tracking software and the entire accounting system.

Part of this candidate's summary might read as follows.

GOOD EXAMPLE:

Detail-oriented accounting professional with six years' experience at a high-volume firm. Proven background partnering with vendors for software upgrades.

The summary statement just gives a high level overview. You'll notice that it didn't specifically mention the $200k in sales. Generally, you'll leave those kinds of details for the Professional Experience section which we'll learn about later-on.

The Summary of Qualifications is also a great place to throw in some of the key skills listed as required or desired qualifications in the job posting. One example might be your computer skills. Let's say the job posting required proficiency in Microsoft Office. If the Junior Accountant was really comfortable using Microsoft Office as well as her company's accounting software, part of her summary might read as follows:

Detail-oriented accounting professional with six years' experience at a high-volume firm. Proven background partnering with vendors for software upgrades. Proficient in the use of Microsoft Office and industry-specific software.

The Summary of Qualifications will be the *only* thing that looks like a full paragraph on your résumé. It should **summarize** anything related to how you can be the best person for the job and include the specific requirements from the job posting. Most recruiters start with the Summary of Qualifications if they're only going to read a small portion of your résumé.

Don't include anything in your summary that you don't mention in the rest of your résumé. If the Junior Accountant also raised cattle, but wasn't applying for a ranch job and didn't have any cattle-rearing on her résumé, it wouldn't be appropriate to list those skills.

In the interest of keeping everything relevant and related to the rest of the résumé, I recommend that you **write the Summary of Qualifications LAST**. Come back to it once you have finished the rest of your résumé. I'm just telling you about it now so you can leave a placeholder in your résumé.

Think back to the movie trailer concept. A studio doesn't produce a preview and then create a movie around it, and neither should you. Put a bookmark on this page and come back to it when you're ready.

SIGN TIME

% - Get ready for creative accounting that's 100% fair!

The Summary of Qualifications can not only summarize the highlights of your experience, but it can also reiterate figures from your résumé to show some numbers in new ways. Use percentages in your summary to restate whole numbers from your experience.

For example, if your experience states that you exceeded goals for 22 of the past 24 months, your summary might say something about exceeding goals for 91% of the time for the past two years.

Here's what your résumé might resemble by now:

Your Name
123 Main Street Any City, ST
<u>yourname@ .com</u> – 555-555-5555

OBJECTIVE: Title of the Job

SUMMARY OF QUALIFICATIONS:
(To be filled in later.)

10

THE FOUNDATION

Now your résumé is really starting to take shape! In this chapter we'll lay down some ground rules that will be the foundation of your entire résumé. We'll talk about 1) the mental foundation or mindset you should adopt before writing a résumé, 2) choosing the right type of résumé to showcase your abilities and 3) the actual format for the information you'll include. As we lay the foundation, keep looking for ways to include the Signs of a Great Résumé. Also keep in mind everything we've already reviewed, for example, a résumé is not a job description.

Here's a few general notes to think about throughout this section:

1: NEVER falsify a résumé.

Doing so could remove you from consideration for a job or could result in your termination if you get the job and your employer finds out later that you lied. You can **<u>fairly</u>** esti- mate some percentages and figures, but **never** lie. When it comes to fairly estimating, ask yourself if you could fairly and accurately describe the information in an interview. If you can and the information is true, include it.

2: Only include information that helps you get hired.

As a general rule, don't list anything on your résumé that doesn't help you to get hired. You've probably filled out job applications that asked for a full work history including every job you've ever done. Résumés are different and require different information and strategies. Since you're in control of the content on your résumé, you can choose to omit periods of unemployment, periods of very brief employment or previous jobs that just aren't relevant to the job for which you are applying. Think again about the hotel ad on TV that we discussed in the chapter "A Résumé Is Not A Job Description." The ad included specific and truthful highlights to entice prospective visitors. The hotel didn't mention that the power went out last year or that the construction going on next door is noisy on some afternoons. Similarly, you should not mention anything less than wonderful on your résumé.

3: Customize your résumé for each job posting.

Any time you apply for a job, you should customize your résumé to match that job's requirements. That's how you make yourself stand out as the strongest candidate. You've likely heard of the theory of natural selection – those with the strongest traits and characteristics are the ones that are most successful in a competitive environment. The same applies to choosing which characteristics from your previous experience should be included on your résumé. When it comes to picking a strong candidate, "survival of the fittest" applies. The employer will chose the applicant who has the characteristics to be the most successful on the job.

So simply put, if you were highly successful in two skills in your last job, and the job you're applying for requires one of the skills but not the other, you should focus on describing the skill that makes you most competitive. People whose résumés don't prove that they have what it takes to survive in a competitive environment will quickly find their career path on the endangered species list, or worse... extinct.

Types of Résumés

There are almost as many different types of résumés as there are colors of the rainbow and then some. The two most common types of résumés are chronological and functional. Don't get too worried about the differences between the two. I'm about to simplify it for you:

Chronological:

This is the more traditional approach to writing a résumé. It's a listing of your experience starting with your most recent job and going backwards to your earliest experience. It's great for those who have had a traditional career path with consecutive employment in reputable establishments.

Functional:

This is a format used when your experience doesn't directly tie-in to the job for which you're applying or when your career path has been less than "traditional."

For example, imagine you were an officer in the military and your unit constructed bridges overseas. You feel you are qualified to manage a department at a manufacturing plant. Because it's not necessarily obvious how those two jobs are related, a chronological résumé might not serve you well. If you're jumping from building bridges to leading an assembly line, there's not a direct connection between the two roles that's easy to see. Leading a team, reading plans and blue prints and delivering results on-time and on-budget are all skills that apply to both jobs. But a recruiter might not easily draw the connection between the two. In order to stand out as a great candidate, you'll need to focus more on the specific skills you learned and the results that you achieved.

A functional résumé is also effective when something doesn't quite add up with the dates you were employed, the names of the jobs you had or the places you worked. To ensure that things like this don't distract a recruiter from your great skills and achievements, that information can get tucked into the bottom of the résumé instead. We'll talk about that later-on in the "Résumé Malfunction?" chapter.

Functional résumés are also commonly used by people who are entrepreneurs, those who flip houses, are independently wealthy, homemakers or who work for a guy named "Lefty" out of the back room of a bar. In other words any "non-traditional" job where a recruiter might not see the benefit of the skills you obtained and how they qualify you for the job opening.

If you're not sure which format to use, start with chrono-logical and go back later if necessary. If you already know you need a functional résumé skip to the chapter entitled "Résumé Malfunction?"

There are a few other types of résumés out there that you probably don't really need to worry about like "blended résumé" (a.k.a. The Freestyle – *Write whatever you want wherever you want it.*) or a curriculum vitae (a.k.a. CV - *Used by doctors, college professors, and European folks*) and my least favorite, the Federal Résumé, (*government bureaucracy at its best.*) I don't recommend any of these formats. Seldom do they serve an applicant's best interests or showcase an applicant's skills. No matter what format you choose, using the Signs of a Great Résumé will make your résumé speak for itself.

Professional Experience Formatting

Let's get into the "meat and potatoes" of the résumé, your previous experience. Your professional experience is the foundation upon which the rest of your résumé is built.

I prefer to title this portion of the résumé **Professional Experience.** Some people call this section Employment History but that doesn't completely capture the essence of what you're going to convey. You're not just going to be talking about your work history. You'll be relaying to your recruiter the highlights of your entire career.

Here's the basic format I use for all portions of the Professional Experience section:

Job Title #1   Feb. 2010 to Present
ABC Company – Any City, ST
• List relevant experience that contains some !@#$%.
• List some more relevant experience with !@#$%.

Job Title #2   Mar. 2003 to Feb. 2010
XYZ Company – Any City, ST
• Again, list relevant experience that contains !@#$%.
• Remember that this section and all sections on your résumé should <u>not</u> read like a job description.

Note that the job title is bolded to draw attention to it. The dates are shown with the abbreviated format of months. If you don't show the months you worked, it can sometimes look like you're trying to hide gaps in employment. Most recruiters won't be nearly as concerned with the dates as you are, so list the months even if your dates don't exactly match up. Be prepared to honestly answer any interview questions about gaps in your employment history.

When you type the name of the company you worked for, you don't have to add corporate structure information like "Inc." "Co." or "LLC" at the end of the company name. It's usually unnecessary and takes up real estate on your résumé. If your company is not well-known, or it has an ambiguous name, you should explain the nature of the business it does somewhere in the first bullet.

GOOD EXAMPLE:

Automotive Sales Manager   Apr. 2008 to Feb. 2011
Joe Bob and Sons – Any City, ST
•   Led a team of 25 associates at this DeLorean dealership.

The first line of this statement has achieved several things. We already know how many people the candidate managed, what kind of company John Doe and Sons is and what specific type of car was sold. All of this was achieved in just ten words and with the Signs of a Great Résumé.

Create an Outline First

Now that you know the format for your Professional Experience, where do you start? Create an outline. Start by listing the titles of the jobs, companies and dates first before anything else. This gives a framework for the entire Professional Experience section and will make it a little easier to organize your thoughts. You'll also be able to determine if you've got all of your dates lined up. Even if you're not sure of the dates of employment, your last employer will usually keep that information in your personnel file for many years after you leave. Call them up and find out what dates you worked there.

Your résumé should look like this by now:

Your Name
123 Main Street Any City, ST
<u>yourname@ .com</u> – 555-555-5555

OBJECTIVE: Title of the Job
SUMMARY OF QUALIFICATIONS:
(To be filled in later.)

PROFESSIONAL EXPERIENCE:

Job Title #1   Feb. 2011 to Present
ABC Company – Any City, ST
•

•

Job Title #2   Mar. 2003 to Feb. 2011
DEFG Company – Any City, ST
•

•

Job Title #3   May 1999 to Feb. 2003
HIJK Company – Any City, ST
•

•

Now that you've got your outline in place, you've laid the foundation for a great résumé. We'll start building upon that foundation in the next chapter.

11

SELF-INTERVIEW

By now you've heard me mention this "Self-Interview" chapter several times throughout the book. The Self-Interview in this chapter is a type of questionnaire that I've developed based on my experience to help you choose the best information to include in the Professional Experience section of your résumé.

By using the questions in this chapter and the Self-Interview Worksheet included in the back of the book, you'll be able to reflect on all the accomplishments and experiences in your career so far. In a way, it's going to be just like looking into a mirror. We'll take a close look at your greatest features and make your résumé look its best.

What Do I Include?

You shouldn't really need to ask this question at this point, but in case you're wondering "What information should I include in the Self-Interview Worksheet?"... the answer of course is !@#$%, the Signs of a Great Résumé!

A Self-Interview Worksheet has been included for your convenience at the back of this book. Just flip to those pages and fill out your answers. Don't worry about spoiling the end of this book by flipping to the last chapter. We already know how the story ends. If you use the Signs of a Great Résumé, your résumé will speak for itself and you'll end up with a great new job!

Once you write down your answers, you'll have them available forever for future reference. Keep this book and your answers handy each time you revise your résumé. Do your best to use !@#$% in your responses. If you need to refresh your memory on the Signs of a Great Résumé, go back to the chapter titled "Sign Language."

Don't worry about the exact phrasing of your responses – We'll cover that in the next chapter "What the !@#$% Should You Say?" For now you're just going to focus on collecting the facts that will help make your résumé speak for itself.

Read through the questions for the Self-Interview here. Once you understand what information to look for, flip to the last chapter and record your answers in the space provided.

1: What were your **key** responsibilities? Just list the basic, most important things you did every day, remembering of course that **A RÉSUMÉ IS NOT A JOB DESCRIPTION!** Don't spend a lot of time on this, just think about things that made your job unique or most interesting. Write one or two lines for your answer to this, but not more. Pay particular attention to the key responsibilities that you can describe with #s and other Signs of a Great Résumé.

2: What did you do that was different than almost everyone else who held the same position? What were your ! moments or accomplishments? How did you stand out from the crowd? Why were you the best at your job? What # ranking did you hold among your peers?

3: How was your specific company better than or different than a similar company elsewhere? How did your company stand out as a ! in the industry? @ which sites and @ what # of sites did you operate?

4: Did you experience or lead something unique? Was it a significant special project, campaign, event, convention, activity or trade show? Describe it. What were the results? How big was the $ it generated? What # people benefitted from it? What kind of exposure and ! did it lead to for your company? What revenues or results did it produce?

5: Did you do something extraordinary that went beyond your normal areas of responsibility? What made it so ! that it was unique?

6: Have you received any awards or commendations for your service, work or technical skills? What kind of ! achievements have you had? Do not include awards for your tenure such as company anniversary awards. How long you spent in a job is already covered in the dates you've listed in your out-line, so there's no need to call additional attention to it here.

7: Do you have any financial data or other metrics that dem-onstrate your success? Do you know how much $ you gen-erated? How much $ did your work save for your company? Can you prove how effective you were with a % of increase or decrease? Was there an efficiency that you can prove with hard facts and data?

8: Did you perform public speaking or mass communication of any kind? Did you conduct a seminar, hold a class, lead a meeting at a civic organization or star in an advertisement or press release for your company? Did you write a national article, a series of blogs or other publications? @ what locations did you speak? What # of people did you reach? What $ did that engagement bring in for your company?

9: What # of customers, students, colleagues or clients did you interact or correspond with daily, monthly or annually on the phone, in-person or online? Did that # grow during your time in the job? What makes that # significant?

Lastly and perhaps most importantly…

10: **What were your greatest contributions to your company?** This is your opportunity to include any achievements, accomplishments or accolades that contributed significantly to your success in your previous jobs which were not covered in the questions above. Pay particular attention to any contributions that contain some !@#$% examples.

The answers to these questions will help you identify which facts to include to make your résumé speak for itself. You'll stand out from the competition when you include this detailed information. Most people will not start their résumé writing process with this much detail, unless they've also smartly purchased this book. Even if you're competing with other applicants who are using the Signs of a Great Résumé, your responses to these questions will be unique to your individual experience.

You've probably guessed that you're not going to be able to fit all of this great content onto your résumé. To quickly catch a recruiter's eye and to ensure you're only listing the best parts of your experience, you need to narrow down what you include. Go back through your answers and select just three to four responses to list under each job. But how do you identify which three responses to include? Let me tell you.

Applying for a job is a bit like trying to pass an exam. You have to study for the exam which you've done by reading this book. You then have to provide the correct answers to the questions on that exam. The "answers" that an employer is looking for are already included in the job posting. They're the "desired" and "required" qualifications listed in the posting. The posting is your "answer key" to the job application exam. Simply identify the responses from the self test that you completed in this chapter which most closely match the answer key. Your top three answers should be related to the desired qualifications and should have some sort of !@#$% in them. If you align your answers from the self test with the answer key, you're sure to ace the exam!

Keep all of the answers that you wrote somewhere safe. That way as you apply for different jobs, you don't have to start from scratch. This self test will be your "study guide" for future job application exams. You're on your way to the head of the class.

12

WHAT THE !@#$% SHOULD YOU SAY?

How Do I Phrase It?

Putting words to paper is often the tough part, but don't fret. I'm going to simplify this for you. Think about the earlier chapter, "Résumés Are Blind – They Have No I's." Go back and re-read that chapter if necessary. I won't put words in your mouth, but I'll at least help you to put the first word into each line of your résumé.

All of your facts for each job will be bulleted. Most of your fragments under each job will start with words known as "action verbs."

Here are a few of my favorite action verbs broken down by the types of things they describe. Each of these is a suitable word for the beginning of a fragment. They're creative, eye catching and lead to !@#$%. Remember, I encourage you to phrase everything in the past tense and you'll see that indicated here.

Communicating:

Consulted, Drafted, Engaged, Influenced, Interacted, Presented, Promoted, Proposed, Researched, Translated, Wrote

Creativity:

Created, Conceived, Designed, Developed, Devised, Drafted, Engineered, Established, Improved, Innovated, Invented, Organized, Pioneered, Performed, Sculpted, Updated

Finance:

Accounted for, Allocated, Audited, Budgeted, Calculated, Drove, Earned, Estimated, Financed, Formulated, Invested, Projected, Raised

Fixing Problems and Finding Efficiencies:

Adjusted, Analyzed, Changed, Completed, Converted, Diagnosed, Discovered, Eliminated, Examined, Executed, Identified, Maximized, Minimized, Planned, Prepared, Recommended, Reconciled, Resolved, Simplified, Solved, Streamlined, Verified

Leadership:

Achieved, Administered, Coached, Delegated, Directed, Evaluated, Founded, Generated, Initiated, Implemented, Judged, Led, Managed, Motivated, Negotiated, Persuaded, Provided, Recruited, Supervised *(My least favorite is "supervised"* since it starts to sound like a job description. Anyone can supervise – you should lead.)

Research:

Analyzed, Assessed, Compared, Compiled, Defined, Organized, Researched, Surveyed

Technical:

Assembled, Built, Constructed, Engineered, Inspected, Installed, Maintained, Manufactured, Mapped, Operated, Programmed, Tested

Training:

Demonstrated, Developed, Exercised, Evaluated, Facilitated, Instructed, Mentored, Partnered, Taught, Tutored, Trained

Working On a Team or In A Group:

Advised, Assisted, Benchmarked, Collaborated, Counseled, Engaged, Facilitated, Helped, Partnered

Now that you have the first word for each sentence, just fill in the blanks. Simply mix an action verb with an appropriate response from your Self Test (as discussed in the previous chapter) and put it on paper. Here are some real-life examples from real résumés written using the Signs of a Great Résumé approach.

Leadership:

- Directed operations for over 20 associates in a 30,000 square foot warehouse.
- Led and coached 10 employees at four sites across the country.
- Expanded operations from a twelve person organization to a workforce of fifty six employees.
- Organized seven leadership conferences and three annual conventions as well as two dozen training programs.
- Instructed a team of 9 associates from diverse backgrounds.
- Awarded with commendation for "Best Performance Of The Year" among 200 associates.

Customer Service and Sales:

- Provided customer service and financial consulting to approximately 25 clients daily, on the telephone and through written communication.

- Succeeded in maintaining strong level of service in this high volume call center, which responded to over 3 million calls annually for 75 unique products and services.
- Represented winery to customers and vendors at 12 major tradeshows throughout the state.
- Responded to over 50 inbound calls daily and provided one-on-one coaching for travel agents from around the country.
- Exceeded sales performance quotas consistently, frequently selling over 40 new subscriptions weekly.
- Attended industry trade shows to drive incremental retail sales with a value of over $14 million.
- Grew direct mail sales 40% annually for each of the last three years in a stagnant segment.

Finance and Revenues:

- Prepared daily cash deposits in excess of $25,000.
- Led a department of twelve associates in successful debt collection, with annual collections totaling nearly $2 million.
- Increased personally-generated profits by 100% in 2009 and 200% in 2011.
- Processed paperwork and monetary transactions over $5 million annually and creatively resolved client dispute issues.
- Collected an average of $150k from accounts 30 to 90 days overdue, the highest results in a company of over 500 employees.
- Coordinated multiple projects and compiled data including expense reports and invoices over $10,000.

- Increased revenues from $300k to $12 million annually.
- Maintained records for $15 million in revenue annually.

Human Resources:

- Performed clinical assessments and developed multi-disciplinary treatment plans for over 100 patients.
- Taught Human Services courses to over 30 classes in public city high schools.
- Provided human resources leadership and insight to 30 leaders at this nationally acclaimed provider of student housing.
- Advised executive leaders on employee relations during a large-scale organizational restructure and outsourcing of nearly 100 jobs.
- Conducted over 50 job evaluations and developed and delivered human resources-related initiatives.
- Reduced lengths of absences 10% by conducting a thorough analysis of the employee health care plan.

Efficiency:

- Developed a best practice program utilizing computer software to improve efficiency of the collections process by as much as 50%.
- Produced savings of approximately $100,000 annually by creating a system which prevented duplicate payments to 38 vendors.
- Efficiently managed cargo flow of over 500 containers monthly from international ports.

71

- Reduced travel expense reimbursement costs by 25% through development of a consistent process and by curtailing expenditures.
- Increased efficiency of contract signing and billing, reducing unsigned contracts by 57%.
- Developed a nationally accredited award program enabling the company to train its own assessors and save nearly $40,000 annually.

Support and Training:

- Trained over 50 new associates in this high volume food service location.
- Designed and operated an extensive European automotive sales website, supporting 17 different dealerships.
- Secured benefits and home support services for a caseload of approximately 75 clients.
- Prepared bank statements, employee garnishments, bookkeeping and time records for approximately 100 clients.
- Conducted 3 unique introductory accounting training courses for undergraduate studies at a community college.
- Acted as a liaison between nearly 300 operators and 200 personnel, coordinating all inventory.
- Responded to over 50 inbound customer inquiries daily for a local and long-distance landline phone provider.
- Resolved over 45 daily computer and labor issues for management over the telephone and in-person.

Use the general ideas and phrasing behind some of these examples and plenty of your own !@#$%, and you'll be on your way to landing that next job. To ensure you're getting your point across succinctly, keep each statement on two lines or less. This will help to quickly catch a recruiter's eye. Lastly, even though these are fragments and not complete sentences, always include a period at the end of each line to show you're done making your point. Period.

SIGN TIME

- Estimate numbers, but do so fairly and accurately. Anything you do daily, can usually be multiplied by 5 work days per week to give you a larger weekly figure.

Anything you do weekly can be multiplied by 50 (figuring in two weeks of vacation) to show *approximately* how much you do in a year.

Anything you do monthly can be multiplied by 12 to estimate what you accomplish in a year.

This means the $500 cash you handle nightly is more like $125k per year and the 100 phone calls you answer per day are actually 500 per week.

Using numbers to describe your experience adds up to some great content for your résumé.

WHAT THE !@#$% SHOULD YOU SAY?

13

BEING SMART ABOUT YOUR EDUCATION

How big a part your education plays on your résumé depends mostly on how big a part it's played in your career. There are a few potential scenarios here.

1. You just graduated from college and have little or no work experience.
2. You have applied what you learned in school directly to your job.
3. You work in a specialized field like accounting, education, engineering, healthcare, information technology, law or a technical field that requires a certain level of education.
4. You have earned an advanced degree or are currently working on one, such as a graduate or doctorate degree.

If any of these scenarios apply to you, then your education section should immediately follow your summary of qualifications.

However, if any of the following apply to you, then you'll list your education at the bottom of your résumé – or you might just omit it altogether.

1. You have little or no formal education.
2. You have an incomplete college education.
3. You went to college ages ago and haven't used anything you learned from your degree during your career.

By listing your education at the bottom in these scenarios, you're letting your résumé speak for itself. You'll do this by first stating the many accomplishments you included from the Self Test in the chapter "Self Test for Success." If you don't have a formal education or your education is incomplete, there's no point in calling attention to it, so leaving it off altogether is typically the way to go. However you may choose to include an education section, if you took courses that have specifically prepared you for the job for which you're applying, even if you didn't finish school. In that case, phrase it as follows:

Name Of Your College – Coursework completed in Subject #1, Subject #2 and Subject #3.

That is about all you'll need to show you're more qualified than the average high school graduate, without calling too much attention to the fact that you didn't quite get to the whole "graduation" technicality. You may not even need to write that much, but if you're dead set on putting something about college on the page, that should be all that you include.

Now for you graduates out there…

PARENTAL ADVISORY: If mom and dad bankrolled college for you, don't let them take this personally - I'm about to reduce their huge investment to a couple little lines on a plain sheet of paper.

Here's how to include information on each degree earned or each one that is currently in progress:

Name Of Degree: Major - Name of School
Minors, Concentrations or Anticipated Graduation Date: ___

78

That's it. Four to six years (or more) of your life, wrapped up in a handful of words. Put the name of the degree in bold font since it likely is the part of your education that most directly prepared you for a job.

If you've just graduated, or have never worked, you can add some bullets underneath highlighting your course of study, GPA in your major (if it was really good like a 3.75 or higher) and any honors or leadership roles you held.

Unless your graduation date is VERY recent and your work history is lacking or absent, you should not list the year of your graduation. Listing the year may hint at your age and could potentially work against you. Your graduation date should only appear to explain why your work history is brief. You should also omit the date if you went to college a long time ago and your work history is brief because you haven't worked.

Also, if you've attended college, there's really no need to mention your high school education on your résumé. Pretty much anyone who went to college had to go to high school or get a GED first. Thus, a high school education basically a "given" to your recruiter. Since listing it would take up precious real estate, leave it off.

A quick note about the verbiage on your degree. Countless scores of people mess this one up and it irks me to no end. Your degree is **NOT** a *Bachelor's of Science*. Calling your degree a *Bachelor's* is slang and it's just plain wrong. Your degree is "Bachelor of Science" or "Associate of Arts," "Master of Business Administration" or whatever the university brass decided to write on the fancy piece of paper in the leather-bound folder collecting dust at your parents' house. Don't believe me? Go read it and give your parents a kiss when I'm right. There is no apostrophe in the name of your degree.

Similarly, do not state that you earned an M.A., B.A., A.A., or the worst two-letter combination: B.S. Your résumé should be factual without any "B.S." anywhere, including in the education section. Why should your recruiter, have to decipher your qualifications when you can simply spell them out? Your goal is to save the recruiter time, not you.

One more quick note. Recruiters really don't care what fraternity or sorority you were in. If you held a leadership role in your Greek organization, AND the group accomplished something amazing with you at the helm, AND what was accomplished is related to the job for which you're applying, then you can include it. You can list that type of experience in a format similar to the other professional experience on your résumé. Beyond that unless you're applying for a job at the national headquarters of your Greek organization, leave your three-lettered family out of it.

Certainly you may have learned a thing or two about networking or another skill in a fraternity or sorority. Heck, you may even luck out and be interviewed by someone who was in the same group! Talking about that experience might be appropriate in an interview if you recognize there's a connection. Use your listening and observation skills to judge whether it's appropriate. You'll read more about that in Signs of a Great Interview... once I write that book. Just leave it off of your résumé.

By now your résumé should look something like this:

Your Name
123 Main Street Any City, ST
<u>yourname@ .com</u> – 555-555-5555

OBJECTIVE: Title of the Job

SUMMARY OF QUALIFICATIONS:
(To be filled in later.)

EDUCATION:
Bachelor Of Science: Major - Any Place University
Minors, Concentrations or Honors

PROFESSIONAL EXPERIENCE:

Job Title #1   Feb. 2009 to Present
ABC Company – Any City, ST
•   Lots of facts and !@#$%.
•   Some more great information and !@#$%.

Job Title #2   Mar. 2002 to Feb. 2009
DEFG Company – Any City, ST
•   Even more accomplishments and !@#$%.
•   And yes, some more highlights of your career sprin-
     kled with !@#$%.

You can now go back and write your Summary of Qualifications. Be sure to highlight some of the items in your résumé, but don't just copy and paste. Summarize them… hence the name of the section. For more help on this section, re-read the chapter entitled "Coming Soon To A Résumé Near You."

Once you've completed your Summary of Qualifications, proofread and spell-check everything. If it all looks good, contains great examples of !@#$% and ties your experience to the job for which you're applying, then congratulations… YOU'RE DONE! You've finished your paper résumé and you're ready to start applying. Read on for more information on additional steps for success. For some thoughts about what you may think is missing from your résumé, advance to the next chapter entitled "Did I Forget Something? …No!"

14

DID I FORGET SOMETHING? ...NO!

Now I know some of you are thinking "Scott, you forgot something that I really think I should include on my résumé." You're probably wondering where to include references, your personal interests, your salary or that lovely little hobby you do on the weekends. These items and more are all examples of things that you should <u>not</u> include on your résumé, with rare exception.

I specifically omitted these items from the résumé writing process for a few reasons, and you should probably omit them too. Now I know that you've likely seen some of these on conventional résumés and you may have included these on an earlier version of your résumé. Just because something is conventional or typical, doesn't make it necessary, effective or correct to include.

I've reviewed lots and lots of candidates as a recruiter so I know what recruiters are looking for on a résumé. We're looking for

hard facts and proof that you're qualified to fill the open position. You've already accomplished this, since you've drafted a
résumé that speaks for itself using the Signs of a Great Résumé.
Other stuff that doesn't really help you to get a job may in fact
hurt your chances. And remember, you don't want anything
taking up valuable real estate on your résumé. Let's learn more.

References Available Upon Request

One of the silliest lines in résumé-writing history has got
to be "References Available Upon Request." Your recruiter
knows that you will furnish references upon request if you
really want the job being offered. DO NOT say "References
Available Upon Request" anywhere on your résumé. It
wastes space and time. You don't say "Interview Available
Upon Request," do you? No. It's a given you'll interview
when asked and you'll also provide references when asked.

I'm not saying don't have references. Just don't waste real
estate on your résumé saying that you do. References help
a recruiter know that you have people who will vouch for
your qualifications. However, recruiters seldom actually call
references. References are a bit of a "stacked deck." You're
obviously only going to pick people who will say wonder-
fully flattering things about you. So there's not a whole lot
of value in a recruiter speaking with them.

If during the job posting process, you are asked for references directly, of course you should provide them. If you
don't have references, you need to straighten that out now
and find some. Have at least three to five work-related

references available. Your family members, your friends and people you knit or worship with are NOT good references, unless they happen to be your boss as well.

It's very important that you get permission from someone before including him or her as a reference. It's also a good idea to have a quick chat with your references about the job for which you're applying. Discuss with them how you're qualified for the role. Ask them if they can recall specific examples of how you demonstrated these qualifications when you worked with them. If you feel like they're well-qualified to sing your praises and they agree to do so, then include them.

List your references on a separate sheet of paper and have it on-hand in an interview, but don't submit it with your résumé. Here's how the references page might look:

Your Name
(555) 555-5555 - yourname@__.com

PROFESSIONAL REFERENCES

John Johnson, Job Title
ABC Company – (555) 555-5555 – email@__.com

Jane Tarzania, Job Title
JKL Company – (555) 555-5555 – email@__.com

Sandy Shoemaker, Job Title
XYZ Company – (555) 555-5555 – email@__.com

Your Company's Fancy Title For The Job You Did

There is absolutely no reason why you must write your job title *exactly* as it appeared on your business card. Remember, the point of a résumé is to convey information quickly and clearly. Using a fancy name to describe a previous job title doesn't achieve that goal. If your recruiter doesn't know what the heck you did, how the heck can he tell you if you're right for the job?

For example, if you were called an AA III and that meant "Advanced Agent Three," neither of those titles help a recruiter understand what you did. Maybe to him, AA III means Acrobatic Aerobics Instructor. Who knows? The point is, if the recruiter doesn't work for your company, he wouldn't have a clue as to what an AA III does.

If being an AA III really means you were an advanced customer sales agent, you could simply write "Advanced Sales Agent." See what I mean? That's much easier to understand. It's more important to convey what you did than what your job was called.

Highly Technical Jargon That Is Industry or Company-Specific

This is similar to the job title concept. If you run the XR4999 at your company and produce micro-carbo-nucleoid-some-thing-or-others, it's unlikely that a recruiter will know what the heck that means. It sounds very complicated and isn't necessary unless you're applying for a job that requires that exact same skill.

If the job for which you're applying doesn't have anything to do with an XR4999, then you'd better help your recruiter out a little bit. Tell them what you did, but keep it short. Explain this in the first bullet listed under that job.

For example, if the XR4999 is one of a few machines you operated, and the micro-carbo-nucleoid-whatevers that it produced are actually air filtering chemicals, you might say "Operated four uniquely complex machines at this global manufacturer of air filtration chemicals." This simple statement helps an uninformed person understand what you do and what your company does with it. Then lay on the !@#$% as heavily as you can to show that you're good at what you do and that you're different than everyone else. Remember to highlight how that experience has prepared you for the job for which you're applying.

When you explain what you did, your recruiter will feel smart about understanding your experience. The smarter the recruiter feels when reading your résumé, the more likely you are to get an interview.

Personal Information

Your résumé should NOT include any of the following tidbits of information, no matter how wonderful of a candidate you think they make you out to be:

- Your birthday
- Your age
- Your social security number
- Your credit score
- Your military rank and pay grade
- Your state of health or disability
- Your religious or political affiliations
- Your ethnicity
- Your familial status (married, single, number of children, etc.)
- Your shoe size (Just in case it crossed your mind...)

If you are reading this book, you are probably not writing a curriculum vitae or a federal résumé. These two documents would require information like a social security number, reference to previous military service and pay grade. A traditional chronological or functional résumé should <u>never</u> include any of this information. There is a time and place for <u>some</u> of this information to be revealed, just never on your résumé. For example, you'll obviously give an employer your social security number when you're hired.

Gory Details

Some people believe that honesty means telling EVERYTHING about yourself on a résumé. I will reiterate that you must be honest, but I will clarify that you should not be **too** honest. DO NOT list any of the following information about your current or past employers on your résumé:

- Your salary
- Your reason for leaving
- Your boss's name, phone number or favorite drink
- Your attendance record
- Your opinion about company performance or policies
- Your review of the company cafeteria

Some jobs themselves fall under the category of "Gory Details" just due to the nature of the job. You may need to do some creative, yet honest revisions to your professional experience to spare your recruiter too many of these gory details. For instance, if you were a cocktail waitress at a strip club it would likely be safe to say you were a "server at a night club" which is far more palatable. If you worked at a place called Joe's Body Piercing House Of Freakin' Unbearable Pain, you might best call it by something else. Maybe there's a more "official" name of the company printed on your paycheck or maybe you can just list the name of your employer as Joe Smith or whatever his name actually is. Perhaps just summarize it as Joe's Body Piercing.

Sometimes leaving the full name of the company out is acceptable, particularly when it could be offensive. Be creative, but be honest.

Hobbies, Extra Curricular Activities and Personal Interests

Allow me to be brutally honest: I don't care what hobbies you do and it's likely that your recruiter doesn't care either. It's lovely that you know how to knit. I'm sure your church appreciates you leading a youth ministry group. Granny probably loves that you take long walks at night with her. But a recruiter is not hiring your sweater, your preacher or your Granny. Unless your hobby **directly** relates to the job for which you're applying, **do** **not** talk about it in your résumé.

Let me explain what I mean by "directly" relating to a job. If you are a martial arts instructor and your hobby is Judo but you teach Tae-Kwon-Do, then your Judo hobby is directly related. If you are a daycare provider and you volunteer running the daycare at your place of worship, that is directly related. If you are an HR Professional and you do voiceovers on the side, that is **not** directly related. Get the idea?

The reason you should exclude this information is that it takes up valuable real estate on your résumé. Again, you're only going to include information that helps you to get hired. Though it's true that recruiters want a well-rounded candidate, one with character and experience beyond the office, there's a time and place to share that type of information. That time is in an interview. If you enjoying kayaking and you walk into an interview to find a picture on the recruiter's desk of her forging a river on a kayak, that might be a good personal connection point. But leave your river exploration off of your résumé.

15

RÉSUMÉ MALFUNCTION?

So you've written all of this great information into a nifty chronological format with plenty of !@#$% but you realize there's something that doesn't quite look right. Any of the following things may be causing a résumé malfunction:

- You have long periods of unemployment or you've job-hopped quite a bit.

- You have lots of great experience, none of which seems to relate well to the job for which you want to apply.

- You have great related experience, but it's brief, as in less than three to five years of professional work experience. (This number is subjective, I'll let you be the judge.)

- You were or are an entrepreneur, running your own business on any scale from something home-based or freelance to a major industry.

If any of these apply to you, continue reading here. If these do not apply, skip to the next chapter.

You've determined that a chronological résumé doesn't seem to fit well with your experience. This is certainly not going to help you land a great job now is it? Have no fear! You have not wasted your time and you don't have to start over! You've laid the framework for a functional résumé, we just need to help you "pretty it up" a bit. It's a different type of writing, but you don't have to be William Shakespeare to make it work. In fact, a résumé by any other name would smell as much like paper as a functional résumé would. Now that you've decided whether a functional résumé format is "to be or not to be," let's help you put it to paper.

What Is A Functional Résumé?

Think of a functional résumé as a "Greatest Hits" album from your favorite musical artist. Each artist has a body of work, but there's a few songs that really define what makes them great. A functional résumé will draw on your key skills (your "greatest hits") instead of summarizing your career chronologically.

The following areas will remain unchanged on a functional résumé: name, address and contact information, summary of qualifications and education. Leave those sections alone for now.

1: Create New Skill Sections:

What you will need to change is your professional experience section. Start with this simple exercise. If someone asked you "What are you *really* good at?" how would you respond? What are your greatest hits? Think of three words that describe the things you do best. These three things will be the "functional" parts of your functional résumé.

Use these three skills as headings for three new skills sections of your functional résumé, similar to how you gave each job a separate section on your chronological résumé.

2: Rearrange Achievements and !@#$% Into Each Skill Section:

Next, we'll use the itemized bullets or achievements under each job listing in your chronological résumé and move each into an appropriate skill section. The achievements and bullets you listed in your chronological résumé likely have a natural fit under your three key skills, so moving them over from one format to another should be fairly simple.

If you're having some trouble figuring out what three skills are right for your functional résumé, here's a hint. Look at the job posting. A recruiter has taken a lot of time to type up the desired and required qualifications for the job posting. Take the top three requirements or so and you've likely found what three skills you should be highlighting. If the top three skills required in the posting don't match your top three skills, you probably shouldn't be applying for this job. Keep looking, you'll find one!

Here are some examples of types of skills you might want to use. All of these are words you might find in a job posting:

- Leadership
- Training, Education, Development or Coaching
- Sales or Revenue Generation
- Financial Acumen or Business Savvy
- Building Relationships or Partnering
- Client, Customer or Guest Service
- Technical Expertise
- …and any other core function of job.

These are just a few examples. Remember, the right top three skills to choose are driven by the type of position being filled. Police officers might include Law Enforcement or Physical Fitness Training. An Information Technology professional might include a separate listing for the key systems he or she is most confident working on. A teacher might include the subject he or she teaches, the additional training he or she has undergone and the extra-curricular activities he or she leads.

3: Place Your Work History at the Bottom of the Page:

Move the company names, job titles and dates to the bottom of the page. If you've filled your functional résumé with so much !@#$% that there isn't room at the bottom of the page, you can attach this second page when you post or leave it out to bring to the interview if you're asked. I recommend fitting it all on to one page with the brief work history on the bottom. Here's how that might look:

Your Name
123 Main Street Any City, ST
yourname@ .com – 555-555-5555

OBJECTIVE: Title of the Job

SUMMARY OF QUALIFICATIONS:
Summarize why you're so good at what you do and how that will help the employer. Yaddy, yaddy, yaddy… Proficient in the use of Microsoft Office and industry-specific computer programs.

LEADERSHIP:

- Lots of facts and !@#$%.
- Some more great information and !@#$%.

SALES RESULTS:

- Even more accomplishments and !@#$%.
- And yes, some more highlights of your career sprinkled with !@#$%.

COACHING AND DEVELOPMENT:

- Something about coaching with !@#$%.
- Some great !@#$% about your development skills.

WORK HISTORY:

Senior Account Manager
ABC Company   Mar. 2010 to Present
Junior Account Manager
XYZ Company   Feb. 2006 to Mar. 2010
Account Management Intern
LMN Company   Nov. 2005 to Jan. 2006

If you need to attach a second page, page two might look like this:

Your Name
555-555-5555 - yourname@ .com
Page 2

EMPLOYMENT HISTORY:

Senior Account Manager
ABC Company – Any Town, ST   Mar. 2010 to Present

Junior Account Manager
XYZ Company – Any Town, ST   Feb. 2006 to Mar. 2010

Account Management Intern
LMN Company – Any Town, ST   Nov. 2005 to Jan. 2006

You should definitely write "Page 2" at the top to ensure that if this page is somehow found alone, the recruiter or hiring manager doesn't mistake this rather bleak and barren sheet of paper for the valuable and informative résumé you've worked so hard to create. They'll know they need to look for Page 1 somewhere. Including your contact information again on Page 2 allows them to call you if they can't find Page 1.

You've officially finished your functional résumé. You've built your "Greatest Hits" album and you're headed for the top of the charts.

16

COVER IT UP

A cover letter is often the forgotten step-child of the résumé writing process. That's odd considering a cover letter serves a very important purpose: To tie your experience *directly* to the job for which you're applying. Still, many people don't have one, most applications I've reviewed didn't include one and some job postings don't require one. In fact, some people feel the cover letter is not necessary or that it's optional. Allow me to clarify this misconception:

A COVER LETTER IS NOT OPTIONAL!

Some tight rope walkers might think a net is optional. But if they plummet to the floor, suddenly that net doesn't seem so optional.

A cover letter is your safety net. A résumé might be fine on its own, but you walk a fine line in assuming that the recruiter will understand how your experience relates to an opening. Without a cover letter, even a well-written résumé could fall to the bottom of the pile. It's a delicate balancing act that you don't want to mess up.

You may be thinking "no one reads cover letters." I'll admit it, many recruiters don't read them. But even if you never need to use the safety net of a cover letter, you'll be grateful that it's there. That's because good recruiters will at least forward your cover letter to the hiring manager. There's where the details are of critical importance.

Typically a recruiter will sort through hundreds of résumés and forward a handful of them to the hiring manager. Hiring managers are more likely to read a cover letter since they'll be seeing fewer résumés. It's critical that the hiring manager fully understands how your experience relates to the open position. By reading the cover letter, he or she may also be able to glean information about your writing skills, personality and overall fitness for the role. If you impress the hiring manager, you get an interview and you get a job. It's just that simple.

Before we start writing a cover letter, there's a few things to mention. Unlike your résumé, a cover letter is <u>not</u> "blind." It's ok to use the word "I." Next, space is limited. You'll have to pick carefully what facts from your résumé you'd like to include. A cover letter is never more than one page, and usually not even a whole page. Include too much information and it will never be read by anyone. And finally, always customize your cover letter to each job for which you apply. Don't reuse or copy the same cover letter from one application to another.

The cover letter lays out your intentions very simply:

* Here's who I am.
* Here's what I've done.
* Here's how my experience relates to your opening.
* Here's how I can help your company.
* Here's how you can contact me for an interview.

That's it! It's that simple. …Ok, so it's not necessarily simple, but I'm going to make it simple for you. I've used the same basic cover letter format for lots of résumés with great results. I'm going to give you that format and let you fill in the blanks to make it your own. My comments are in parentheses.

Ready? Let's give it a shot.

GOOD COVER LETTER EXAMPLE:

Your Name
Address
City, ST ZIP
Phone Number
Email Address
    (Use the same header as you did on your résumé. Include all the information that will be necessary to contact you.)

Hiring Manager Name (If Known)
Company Name
Address
City, ST ZIP

Regarding: Job Posting Title
    (Include position number if known)

Dear Hiring Manager,
    (Insert the name of hiring manager or recruiter if known)

Thank you for taking time out of your busy day to review my résumé. I am very excited to be considered for the position of ___(A)___.
(A: The exact title of the job for which you're applying).

I would like to contribute my ___(B)___ years of experience in ___(C)___ to the success of ___(D)___.

(B: Total number of years of your work history)
(C: Your line of work)
(D: The company's name)

Throughout my career I have gained strong expertise in the areas of ___(E)___ and ___(F)___.
   (E & F: List two things you're really good at.)

With my ___(G)___ and attention to detail, the ___(H)___ that I have contributed to have enjoyed ___(I)___.
   (G: List another of your key skills; You should have good attention to detail. If not, go learn it.)
   (H: The companies, schools, organizations, groups, hospitals, etc.)
   (I: How did your prior employers benefit? i.e.- increased revenues, decreased cycle time, improved efficiencies, etc.)

I feel that my experience in ___(J)___ will be of great service to your organization.
   (J: Name of your field – i.e.- sales, HR, IT, education, etc.)

I understand that you are looking for a candidate with ___(K)___.

   (K: Insert part of the job description from the job posting that you feel you are most qualified for here, and explain how you've demonstrated that with something from your résumé.)

Additionally, my communication abilities, both written and verbal, enable me to maintain the confidence of my leaders while growing the loyalty of our clients.

(If for some reason this doesn't apply to you, and it should, then add another part of the job description and describe how your experience relates.)

I have developed my ___(L)___ skills to foster long-lasting relationships with a diverse range of clients, peers, and leaders through creativity, customer support, and proven follow-up skills.

(L: Some kind of people skills – i.e.- partnering, teaching, training, networking, sales, interaction, presentation, etc. Ensure all the elements of the last part of the sentence all apply to you.)

Thank you once again for your consideration. Please feel free to contact me at your earliest convenience so that I may answer further questions regarding my qualifications for this position. I look forward to meeting with you in-person sometime soon.

Very truly yours,
(or Sincerely, Best regards, Fondly, whatever you typically use)

Your Name

That's it! That's your cover letter. Pretty simple, eh?

Here is a real life example. It's a cover letter written for a client of mine for a role in urban infrastructure development and planning.

Here are some of the qualifications from the job posting:

- Minimum 3 years of relevant professional experience;
- Must have excellent oral and written communication skills;
- Must have international experience working in areas related to urban development operations and a passion for urban development;
- Must be able to give help and advice to others based on their specialized area of knowledge and skills in the urban sector;
- Uses technical knowledge and skills to complete complex work relating to urban sector;
- Uses technical knowledge and skills to improve work systems;

Dear Hiring Manager,

Thank you for taking time out of your busy day to review my résumé. I am very excited to be considered for the position of Urban Development Manager. I would like to contribute my 12 years of professional experience in the study and execution of urban development and planning to the success of the National Development Company.

Throughout my career I have gained strong expertise in the areas of transportation engineering, infrastructure

---

management, sustainable development and economic development. With my research skills and attention to detail, the projects that I have contributed to have enjoyed creative solutions to complex social and economic issues. I have also obtained excellent technical knowledge in economics and finance through engagement in the Chartered Financial Analyst program. I feel that my experience in urban planning and economics will be of great service to your organization.

I understand that you are looking for a candidate with a passion for international development. In my experience, I have delivered outstanding results in urban infrastructure development across several continents. I have honed my international relationship skills to foster long-lasting relationships with people of different nationalities and cultural backgrounds. I have accomplished this through creativity, academic excellence, and proven delivery skills in a variety of mediums. Additionally, my written and verbal communication abilities in English, Chinese and German, enable me to communicate with and relate to people across the globe.

Thank you once again for your consideration. Please feel free to contact me at your earliest convenience so that I may answer further questions regarding my qualifications for this position. I look forward to meeting with you in-person sometime soon.

Very truly yours,

Name Of Applicant

You'll notice how none of the information in this letter was copied verbatim from the posting. However, since the applicant drew direct connections between his experience and the required qualifications, it was easy for the hiring manager to see why he was a good fit for the role. This "safety net" helped land him the job.

17

KEEPING ONLINE POSTING IN LINE

Posting your résumé online can either be a rewarding or a frustrating process. The online marketplace has connected employers to thousands of job seekers they couldn't have reached before in newspaper ads or other traditional job posting mediums.

However, it has also connected them to under-qualified, poorly-directed, and money-driven job applicants who never would have applied before the age of the internet. Anyone can now apply for any job and that's not always a good thing for an employer searching for a right-fit candidate who is qualified to perform an open job. It's this flooded landscape that makes using the Signs of a Great Résumé all the more important.

Here's a few tips on how to get the most from posting your résumé online.

ONLINE TIP #1: Calm Down!

Get your trigger finger under control! You are probably not qualified to do every job in a 5, 10 or 15 mile radius from your home, so don't post for everything you see.

You should only consider posting for jobs that at least meet the following qualifications:

DO Post: If you REALLY want that specific job.

Don't post for any other reason. If it's not the job you've been looking for and you haven't previously considered that type of job, DO NOT POST. If you're only looking at the field that says "Salary," DO NOT POST. If you've never heard of the company and don't know anything about it, DO NOT POST. What would happen if you got that job? You'd likely be disappointed after the money stopped being exciting. Your new employer might not be thrilled either.

DO POST: If you are ACTUALLY qualified to do the job.

Picture the job application process in reverse. Have a trusted friend who is well-informed about your work history read you the job posting. Ask your friend if she thinks you can honestly be the **very** **best** person for that job. Ask yourself the same question.

Take a moment and go through each of the desired and required qualifications for the job. Put a check next to the ones you're qualified to do and circle the ones you're for which you're really not qualified. If you've got more circles than checks, your candidacy isn't in such great shape and you should probably keep looking for another posting.

If you do have a lot of the desired and required qualifications, go back to the top and re-read the job description. Can you picture yourself doing this EVERY DAY for the foreseeable future? Don't take a job for the short-term; assume that you'll make a career out of it.

Once you know you **can** do the job and you **want** to do the job, take a look at the company that has posted the job. Go to their website. Research the heck out of them. Read every news article, press release, and employee-written blog you can find. Not only will you keep yourself in check, but this process can also help to prepare for the interview you'll hopefully land by posting for the opening.

ONLINE TIP #2: Customize Your Résumé

You are not fully qualified to do the job in the eyes of the recruiter until your résumé tells them so. Take the job posting and compare it to your résumé. If they don't look somewhat similar, you'll have to make some revisions.

Remember from the "Self-Interview" chapter that applying for a job posting is like completing an exam with open ended questions. The employer has already given you all of the answers. Each of the qualifications and job responsibilities that are listed tells you exactly what the recruiter wants to see on your résumé. Go and make it so!

While you might not be able to copy and paste the information verbatim, (and you shouldn't) you **can** use some of the same terminology and phrasing that the job posting gives you.

Here are some examples:

Posting: Ability to work in a fast-paced operation with little supervision.
Bullet From Your Current Résumé: Managed 12 employees in a high-volume call center environment with over 100 unique products.
Revise Your Bullet To Say: Independently managed 12 employees in a fast-paced call center operation with over 100 unique products.

See how easy that was? I changed a couple of words, used plenty of !@#$% and now this experience ties directly to the posting. Let's see another example:

Posting: Responsible for the acquisition of emerging technology within a strict budget.
Bullet From Your Current Résumé: Purchased software and peripherals with a budget of $15 million annually.
Revise Your Bullet To Say: Acquired emerging technology including software and peripherals, delivering results within the $15 million budget.

Again, all that was necessary was to change a couple of words around and POOF, like magic this experience is directly related to the job posting. Imagine the results if you could do this with a few more of your bullets!

As you can see applying for a job online isn't really all that different than using a traditional paper résumé. The main difference is that the convenience of the online job marketplace allows hundreds if not thousands of more applications to flood a recruiter's desk. That makes it even harder for an applicant to stand out amongst the competition. Because of this, using Signs of a Great Résumé is more important now than ever. Using !@#$% will help you create an online résumé that speaks for itself. As you draft your online résumé, go back through each chapter of this book and apply the same simple principles. Being smart about posting online will land you in line for a great new job.

18

THE FINISH LINE

Congratulations! You are on your way to your next great job!

Pat yourself on the back or ask someone else to do it for you. You've made an important difference in how you will hunt for a job from this point forward. You've learned about what kind of information makes you a strong candidate and what kinds of things drive some recruiters crazy. You've learned how to write a résumé that speaks for itself!

I wish you well on what I'm sure will be a successful job hunt. You don't need to be wished "good luck" because you have more than luck on your side. You have the facts, the format and of course, lots of !@#$% to help you land your next job.

We've come a long way together from a corny joke about two résumés talking in a pile to writing a great new résumé that speaks for itself. Now that you've written the résumé you can finally relax. You can go out and post with confidence for jobs that you are qualified to do. You can also revel in the fact that while others paid someone like me hundreds of dollars to write a résumé for them, you did it yourself and only paid me a fraction of that price for this nifty little book.

Perhaps you'll get the first job you apply for with your new résumé. Perhaps recruiters everywhere will smile as they start to see more résumés with the Signs of a Great Résumé included. Perhaps you'll tell all of your friends to go out and buy this book. (Pretty please.) But without a doubt your résumé is stronger and future recruiters will thank you for being specific, concise and well-prepared. For now, best wishes and happy job hunting! I'll see you out there, and you'll see me... on the back of my next book, Signs of a Great Interview. Keep an eye out for it! All the best.

SELF-INTERVIEW WORKSHEET

Once you've read through the Self-Interview chapter, use the space provided on the following pages to fill in answers to these questions. Be sure to list responses for each job that you've held. Remember, the strongest answers will use the Signs of a Great Résumé, so try to include as much !@#$% as you can.

1: What were your key responsibilities? Just list the basic, most important things you did every day, remembering of course that A RÉSUMÉ IS NOT A JOB DESCRIPTION! Don't spend a lot of time on this, just think about things that made your job unique or most interesting. Write one or two lines for your answer to this, but not more. Pay particular attention to the key responsibilities that you can describe with #s and other Signs of a Great Résumé.

_____

_____

_____

_____

_____

_____

SELF-INTERVIEW WORKSHEET

_____

_____

_____

_____

_____

_____

_____

_____

_____

_____

_____

_____

_____

_____

_____

_____

2: What did you do that was different than almost everyone else who held the same position? What were your
! moments or accomplishments? How did you stand out
from the crowd? Why were you the best at your job? What #
ranking did you hold among your peers?

_____

_____

_____

_____

_____

_____

_____

_____

_____

_____

_____

_____

SELF-INTERVIEW WORKSHEET

_____

_____

_____

_____

_____

_____

_____

_____

_____

_____

_____

_____

_____

_____

3: How was your specific company better than or different than a similar company elsewhere? How did your company stand out as a ! in the industry? @ which sites and @ what # of sites did you operate?

_____

_____

_____

_____

_____

_____

_____

_____

_____

_____

_____

_____

SELF-INTERVIEW WORKSHEET

4: Did you experience or lead something unique? Was it a significant special project, campaign, event, convention, activity or trade show? Describe it. What were the results? How big was the $ it generated? What # people benefitted from it? What kind of exposure and ! did it lead to for your company? What revenues or results did it produce?

_____

_____

_____

_____

_____

_____

_____

_____

_____

_____

_____

_____

SELF-INTERVIEW WORKSHEET

_____

_____

_____

_____

_____

_____

_____

_____

_____

_____

_____

_____

_____

_____

_____

5: Did you do something extraordinary that went beyond your normal areas of responsibility? What made it so ! that it was unique?

_____

_____

_____

_____

_____

_____

_____

_____

_____

_____

_____

_____

_____

SELF-INTERVIEW WORKSHEET

_____

_____

_____

_____

_____

_____

_____

_____

_____

_____

_____

_____

_____

_____

_____

_____

6: Have you received any awards or commendations for your service, work or technical skills? What kind of ! achievements have you had? Do not include awards for your tenure such as company anniversary awards. How long you spent in a job is already covered in the dates you've listed in your outline, so there's no need to call additional attention to it here.

_____

_____

_____

_____

_____

_____

_____

_____

_____

_____

_____

_____

SELF-INTERVIEW WORKSHEET

_____

_____

_____

_____

_____

_____

_____

_____

_____

_____

_____

_____

_____

_____

_____

_____

7: Do you have any financial data or other metrics that demonstrate your success? Do you know how much $ you generated? How much $ did your work save for your company? Can you prove how effective you were with a % of increase or decrease? Was there an efficiency that you can prove with hard facts and data?

_____

_____

_____

_____

_____

_____

_____

_____

_____

_____

_____

_____

_____

_____

_____

_____

_____

_____

_____

_____

_____

_____

_____

_____

_____

_____

8: Did you perform public speaking or mass communication of any kind? Did you conduct a seminar, hold a class, lead a meeting at a civic organization or star in an advertisement or press release for your company? Did you write a national article, a series of blogs or other publications? @ what locations did you speak? What # of people did you reach? What $ did that engagement bring in for your company?

_____

_____

_____

_____

_____

_____

_____

_____

_____

_____

_____

SELF-INTERVIEW WORKSHEET

_____

_____

_____

_____

_____

_____

_____

_____

_____

_____

_____

_____

_____

_____

_____

9: What # of customers, students, colleagues or clients did you interact or correspond with daily, monthly or annually on the phone, in-person or online? Did that # grow during your time in the job? What makes that # significant?

_____

_____

_____

_____

_____

_____

_____

_____

_____

_____

_____

_____

_____

SELF-INTERVIEW WORKSHEET

_____

_____

_____

_____

_____

_____

_____

_____

_____

_____

_____

_____

_____

_____

Lastly and perhaps most importantly…

10: **What were your greatest contributions to your company?** This is your opportunity to include any achievements, accomplishments or accolades that contributed significantly to your success in your previous jobs which were not covered in the questions above. Pay particular attention to any contributions that contain some !@#$% examples.

_____

_____

_____

_____

_____

_____

_____

_____

_____

_____

_____

SELF-INTERVIEW WORKSHEET

_____

_____

_____

_____

_____

_____

_____

_____

_____

_____

_____

_____

_____

_____

_____

NOTES:

NOTES:

_____

_____

_____

_____

_____

_____

_____

_____

_____

_____

_____

_____

_____

_____

_____

NOTES:

NOTES: